AN ALPHABET OF ANGELS

An Alphabet of

ANGELS

NANCY WILLARD

THE BLUE SKY PRESS

An Imprint of Scholastic Inc. · New York

The Blue Sky Press

Copyright © 1994 by Nancy Willard

All rights reserved.

For information regarding permission, please write to:
Permissions Department,
The Blue Sky Press, an imprint of Scholastic Inc.,
555 Broadway, New York, New York 10012

The Blue Sky Press is a trademark of Scholastic Inc.

Library of Congress Cataloging-in-Publication Data
Willard, Nancy.
An alphabet of angels / Nancy Willard.
p.   cm.
ISBN 0-590-48480-X
1. Angels — Juvenile poetry. 2. English language — Alphabet —
Juvenile literature. 3. Alphabet rhymes. [1. Angels — Poetry.
2. Alphabet. 3. American poetry.] I. Title.
PS3573.I444A82   1994   811′.54 — dc20   [E]   93-48836   CIP   AC
12 11 10 9 8 7 6 5 4 3 2 1   4 5 6 7 8 9/9
Printed in Singapore
First printing, September 10, 1994

FOR JAMES AND JULIE

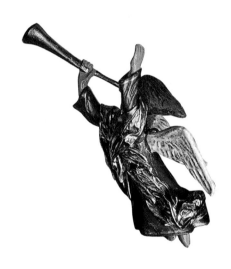

Every blade of grass has over it an angel saying, "Grow."

— THE TALMUD

The angel of alphabets opens the door.

Our △ aim should be, I think, to make letters live:

The book angel whispers, "Go out and explore."

C

The angels of chimneys sing to the sweep.

The angel of dreaming flies in her sleep.

The angel of eggs repeats to the shell:
What's still as a secret and clear as a well?

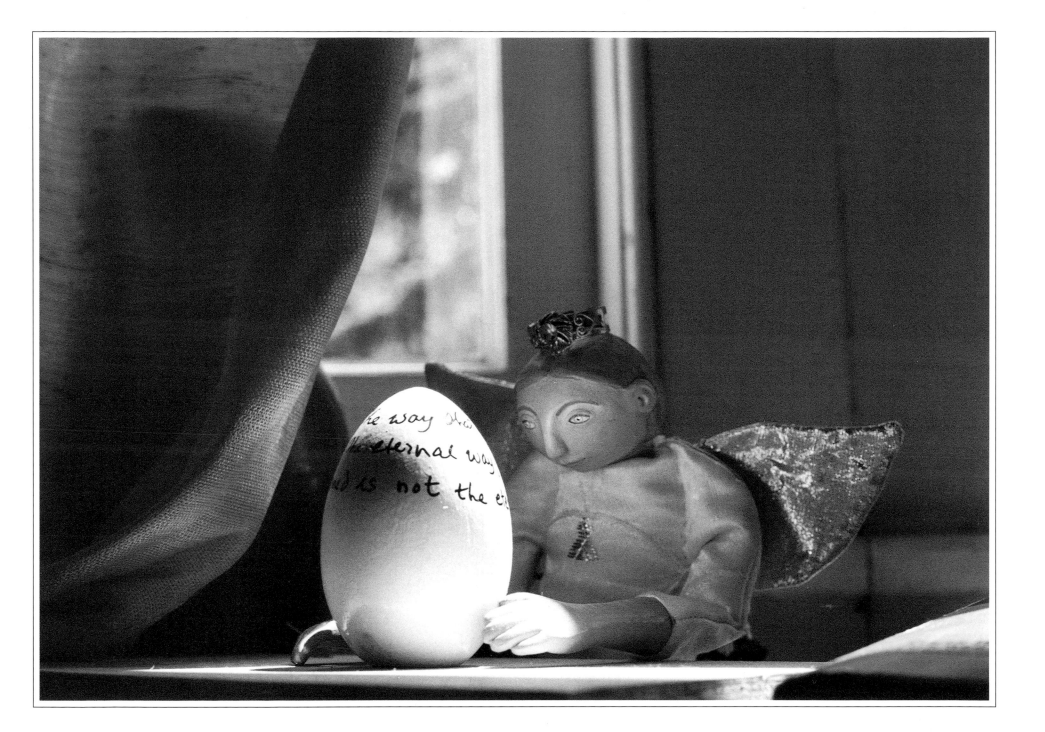

The angels of flowers have startled the grass.

The angel of games lets nobody pass.

The angel of halos gives up her gold bands.

The angel of ink is the servant of hands.

The angel of journeys is friend to the fish.

The angel of knapsacks delivers a wish

L

to the angel of letters, unfolding like lace

when the angel of morning wears dew on his face.

The angels of night
crow with delight.

The angel of oranges shakes them all free.

The angel of planets is small as a bee.

The angel of quiet lets visitors go.

The angel of rooftops flies thrillingly low.

The angel of streetlights is polishing roads

for the angel of trumpets — their silence explodes.

The undersea angel leaves shelter behind.

The angel of vegetables ripens a rind.

The angel of windows opens them wide.

The angel of X rays takes us inside.

The angel of yonder looks after the light.

Z

The zodiac angel sings us good night.

Four angels to my bed,
Gabriel stands at the head,
John and Peter at my feet,
All to watch me while I sleep.

— ANONYMOUS